SIERRA CLUB WILDLIFE LIBRARY

SEALS

SIERRA CLUB WILDLIFE LIBRARY

SEALS

Text by Eric S. Grace
Photographs by Fred Bruemmer

General Editor, R. D. Lawrence

Sierra Club Books
San Francisco

Little, Brown and Company
Boston • New York • Toronto • London

The Sierra Club, founded in 1892 by John Muir, has devoted itself to
the study and protection of the earth's scenic and ecological resources —
mountains, wetlands, woodlands, wild shores and rivers, deserts and plains.
The publishing program of the Sierra Club offers books to the public as a
nonprofit educational service in the hope that they may enlarge the public's
understanding of the Club's basic concerns. The Sierra Club has some sixty
chapters in the United States and in Canada. For information about how you
may participate in its programs to preserve wilderness and the quality of life,
please address inquiries to Sierra Club, 730 Polk Street, San Francisco,
CA 94109.

First Paperback Edition

All photographs © Fred Bruemmer, except the following: © Donald
Denton / First Light Associated Photographers, 34; © International Fund
for Animal Welfare, 51; © Wayne Lynch, 35, 37, 39; © Carleton Ray /
The National Audubon Society Collection, 13; © Tom Ritchie, 14, 17.

Library of Congress Cataloging-in-Publication Data

Grace, Eric S.
    Seals / text by Eric S. Grace; photographs by Fred Bruemmer. — 1st ed.
        p.   cm. — (Sierra Club wildlife library)
    Summary: Introduces the physical characteristics, habits, and habitats of
seals, sea lions, and walruses.
    Includes index.
ISBN 0-316-32279-2 (hc)
ISBN 0-316-32291-1 (pb)
    1. Seals (Animals) — Juvenile literature. 2. Sea lions — Juvenile
literature. 3. Walruses — Juvenile literature. [1. Seals (Animals) 2. Sea
lions. 3. Walruses.] I. Bruemmer, Fred, ill. II. Title. III. Series.
QL737.P6G73 1991   91-15018
599.74'5 – dc20

Sierra Club Books/Little, Brown children's books are published by Little,
Brown and Company (Inc.) in association with Sierra Club Books.

Published in Canada by Key Porter Books Limited

Printed in Hong Kong

10 9 8 7 6 5 4 3 2 1

Contents

Between Land and Sea   6

Seals of the World   10

Seasons of a Seal   24

Life in the Cold   40

Life in the Deep   48

Underwater Hunters   52

Pinnipeds and People   60

Index   63

Between Land and Sea

Did you ever have the feeling you were being watched? I did, one summer afternoon as I hiked along a rocky ocean beach. I felt sure that a pair of big eyes were staring at me from somewhere. There was a large boulder nearby, so I quickly climbed on top of it to look around. The shoreline was narrow and littered with tumbled rocks and driftwood. On one side was the sea, and on the other was a steep cliff. Halfway up the cliff, a twisted tree trunk clung to the rock face. On one of its dead branches perched a sleeping gull. The only sound I heard was that made by the ocean waves, softly lapping the wet stones.

With a ruffling of its feathers, the gull woke. Seeing me, it gave a harsh call, dropped from its perch, and flew low across the open water. As I followed its flight with my eyes, I suddenly spotted my watcher among the gently bobbing waves.

The dark head that broke the surface of the gray water belonged to a *harbor seal*. At first glance, the seal had looked like a piece of drifting tree trunk, or the top of a submerged rock. But when I watched it closely for a while, the outline of its shape changed as the seal twisted in the water. Then the shape quickly disappeared, only to pop up later a few yards farther away.

Through a pair of binoculars, I got a closer look at the seal's dog-like face with its rounded head, long whiskers, and dark, gentle eyes. The seal was peering back at me curiously. Its dog-like appearance is no accident, for seals are distant cousins of dogs, cats, and other meat-eaters called *carnivores*.

*Harbor seals live close to the
shore, seldom traveling more
than ten miles from the place
where they were born.*

Like their relatives, seals are hunters, or *predators*. Except for a few kinds of seals that live in freshwater lakes, their hunting grounds are the oceans.

The harbor seal rolled over on the water's surface, showing me more of its smooth body. Its streamlined shape, like that of fish and whales, helps the seal move easily through the water. Although I could not follow it beneath the waves, I knew that the seal was a swift and agile diver. It had to be, in order to catch the fish and squid it lived on.

Because seals depend on the sea for their food, they spend much of their lives in the water. Unlike fish and whales, however, seals can leave the sea. They make their home in two very different environments: on land and in the water.

I have seen harbor seals resting on this same beach. Surprisingly, they are sometimes as hard to spot on land as in the water. With their gray or brown coats and irregular dark and light spots, sleeping seals look much like sea-smoothed boulders.

More than 300,000 harbor seals live along the Pacific coast of North America, from Alaska to Baja California. Harbor seals also live along the east coast of North America, from Northern Canada to Cape Cod, as well as along the coasts of Europe and Northeast Asia.

When a seal is on land, you can get a good look at its fin-shaped limbs. Because of the shape of their limbs, biologists call seals *pinnipeds*—meaning "wing- or fin-footed." The seal uses its limbs as paddles or rudders underwater and as legs on land. In addition to resting, pinnipeds also come out of the water to molt (shed their fur), mate, give birth, and nurse their young.

Soon, the harbor seal I was watching swam farther out to sea and I continued my walk along the beach. The seal's world and mine had touched briefly in this place where the ocean meets the land. As I walked, I thought some more about our encounter. Where had this seal come from, and where was it going? What did it do underwater when I could no longer see it? Was it alone, or were other seals nearby, still watching me from places unseen? What could I learn from seals if I could follow them and watch them go about their lives? We are alike in some ways but have developed such different skills to survive on our shared planet earth.

Seals make their home both in the sea and on land.

9

Seals of the World

Like people, seals are *mammals* — warm-blooded, air-breathing animals that suckle their young. There are more than thirty different kinds, or *species*, of pinnipeds altogether, found in oceans, in some freshwater lakes, and along coastlines around the world. All have a streamlined shape and other features that allow them to live in water and on land. Each species, however, differs from the others in appearance and way of life.

Some seals are social and gather in huge herds, while others tend to live alone most of the year. Some spend their lives largely at sea, while others often come onto land. Some seals are noisy, producing bellows, roars, grunts, or barks; others rarely make a sound. Some seals regularly migrate over long distances, and some stay in one area all their lives. In several species, male seals (called bulls) are much bigger than the females (called cows). In other species, bulls and cows are about the same size.

Based on the similarities and differences found among the many species of pinnipeds, biologists have divided them into three groups, known as *families*. The largest family, with the most species, includes the earless seals, or *true seals*. A typical true seal is the harbor seal. The second family contains the sea lions and fur seals, which together are called *eared seals*. The third, and smallest, family consists of just one species — the *walrus*. Whether true seals, eared seals, or walruses, all these mammals are easily recognized as pinnipeds. Just look for the streamlined, flipper-shaped limbs.

PINNIPED ANCESTORS

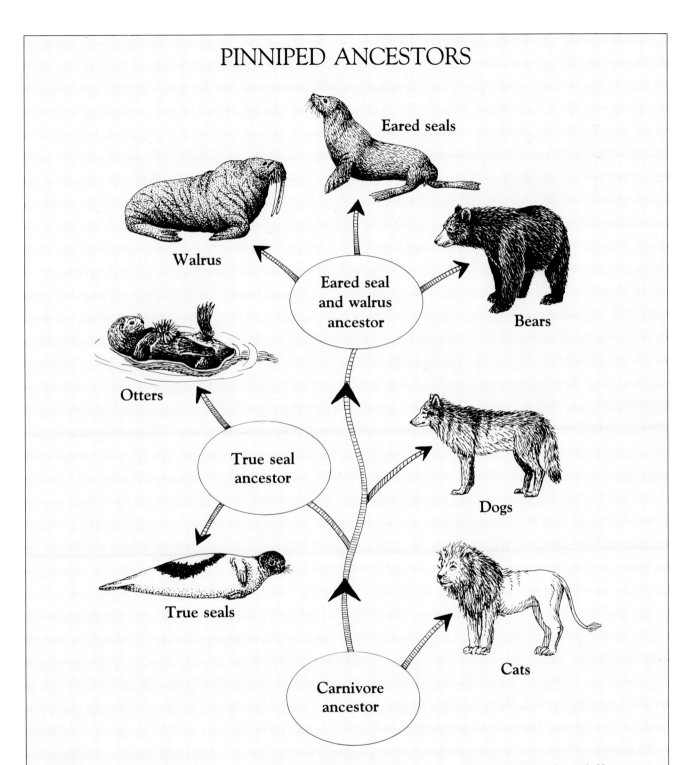

Millions of years ago, the distant ancestors of all pinnipeds lived on land. They were dog-size mammals that hunted their food in forests and swamps. Over hundreds of thousands of generations, these ancient carnivores slowly changed as they adapted to different environments. Fossil remains of early pinnipeds show biologists that the true seals developed from different ancestors than those of eared seals and walruses. The three families also developed at different times. The ancestors of true seals appear to have been otter-like animals. The ancestors of eared seals and walruses, on the other hand, were bear-like.

A true seal has no external ear flap. This is why it is sometimes called an "earless" seal.

TRUE SEALS

There are about four times as many true seals around the world as eared seals. Most live in the cold waters of the far north and south, where their thick blubber and compact shape help them stay warm. The exceptions include two rare species of *monk seals*. One species lives only in the warm waters of the Mediterranean Sea, and the other is found in the Pacific Ocean near the Hawaiian Islands. A third species, the *Caribbean monk seal*, was last seen in 1949 and is now thought to be *extinct* (no longer living anywhere on earth). Monk seals get their name from the fold of skin at the back of their necks, which looks like the hood of a cloak worn by monks.

Both the smallest and the largest pinnipeds in the world are true seals. The smallest seal species is the *ringed seal*, which lives in the cold Arctic seas around the north pole. The dark blotches on its skin are surrounded by paler rings, which give the seal its name. Male ringed seals measure between four and six feet long and rarely weigh more than 250 pounds. Females are about one-third smaller. Ringed seals avoid the open ocean, staying near land or solid ice.

The ringed seal is the smallest species of seal.

The giant of the seal world is suitably named the *elephant seal*. There are two species: northern elephant seals live along the west coast of North America from Baja California to Alaska; the even larger southern elephant seals live in the icy waters of the Antarctic Ocean. A bull southern elephant seal may measure twenty feet from nose to tail and weigh as much as four tons. These truck-size animals can swallow a small shark in one gulp. Because of their huge size, elephant seals have difficulty moving on land. A biologist once timed an elephant seal that he saw arrive at a beach. It took an hour and a half for the animal to drag itself completely clear of the water. It spent most of that time resting from its exertions!

The southern elephant seal is the giant of the seal world.

EARED SEALS

Sea lions and other eared seals do have recognizable ears.

Eared seals do not range as far north or south as true seals. They live along the coasts of Alaska and Siberia in the north, and in the southern seas around South America, Australia, and New Zealand. Many also live in the warmer seas near the equator. Eared seals spend more time on land than do true seals, especially during the breeding season when they are raising their young. Eight of the thirteen species of eared seals have dense undercoats of rich, soft fur; these are called *fur seals*. The other five species, with sparse undercoats and blunter noses, are called *sea lions*.

The bull Steller's sea lion looks massive compared to his mate.

The sleek, playful *California sea lion* zips among the waves, sometimes leaping out of the water like a dolphin. In short bursts, sea lions have been clocked underwater at speeds of twenty-five miles per hour. During summer and fall, the adult male sea lions move away from their breeding grounds off the coast of California, swimming as far as Canada and Mexico in search of food. The females and pups stay near the breeding islands year-round. California sea lions learn quickly and have been trained to do balancing and other tricks in marine shows and circuses.

Among all eared seals, males are much bigger than females. This difference in size is most striking in the *Steller's sea lion*, the largest species of eared seals. Named for scientist Georg Wilhelm Steller, who first described the species in 1742, the Steller's sea lion lives along the Pacific coast of North America from Alaska to southern California. The bulls of this species weigh as much as one ton and are fourteen feet long. The cows are only a quarter that size. Mature bulls, five years old or more, grow lion-like manes around their thick, muscular necks. Steller's sea lions often occupy steep rocky areas along the seashore, where they leave and enter the water in spectacular leaps between the surf and the rocks.

Only one species of fur seal lives north of the equator. The Alaskan or *northern fur seal* spends the winter in the north Pacific Ocean. Then it migrates even farther north each summer to gather in huge colonies off the coast of Alaska. Millions of these seals were killed for their fur during the 1800s, and by 1911 there were fewer than 150,000 left in the world. In recent years herds have been protected, and there are now more than one and a half million northern fur seals. They are one of the most studied and best-known seals in the world.

By contrast, little is known about the fur seals that live south of the equator. They, too, were heavily hunted in the past, and some species are now very rare. The *Guadalupe fur seal* was thought to be extinct in the 1920s, but a small herd was rediscovered in 1954, near the island of Guadalupe, off Baja California. There are probably not more than 500 of these seals living today, but with continued protection and pollution controls, their numbers may increase.

A small population of Guadalupe fur seals lives on the Pacific coast of Central America.

HOW CAN YOU TELL A TRUE SEAL FROM AN EARED SEAL?

True seals have rounded heads and little or no neck. They have no external ear flaps—only tiny ear openings that they can close with their ear muscles. This is why they are sometimes called "earless" seals.

Eared seals have pointed faces and distinct necks. They have small external ears that look like fur-covered tubes. The ears lie close to the eared seal's head and point stiffly backward, helping to keep the animal streamlined.

True seal

Eared seal

True seal

Eared seal

True seal

Eared seal

On land, true seals are "crawlers." They move by arching their bodies and pulling themselves forward with their front flippers. Their rear flippers point backward and are not very useful for walking. Their movement on land looks awkward, but the fastest can "hump" over the ice at speeds of more than ten miles per hour.

Eared seals can walk on land using all four flippers. They are able to turn their long rear flippers and point them forward. They waddle when moving slowly, but break into a lunging gallop when they need to go faster.

Underwater, true seals use their rear flippers for propulsion. When swimming quickly, they press the two flippers against each other, like a person with the palms of the hands held together, and sweep their rear ends from side to side or up and down. They use their front flippers for steering.

Eared seals — especially sea lions — are the speedsters of the seal world. They propel themselves with their front flippers. In order to swim in this way, eared seals have a heavier and more powerful front end than true seals. They use their rear fins as rudders, for steering and balance.

The name "walrus" comes from the Norwegian words meaning "whale horse."

WALRUSES

Like an eared seal, the tusk-toothed, bewhiskered *walrus* can turn its back flippers forward for walking on land. Like a true seal, however, the walrus has no external ears. The walrus is a unique species that cannot be mistaken for any other pinniped. Biologists place it in a family of its own.

Walruses live along the cold northern coasts of both the Atlantic and Pacific Oceans. The most striking thing about a walrus is its huge tusks, which are actually extended canine teeth growing from the animal's upper jaw. Both sexes grow them. In large males, the tusks may be more than two feet long and ten inches around. Baby walruses are born without tusks and must be cared for by their mothers for two years, until their tusks have grown long enough to enable them to look after themselves.

The scientific name of the walrus (*Odobenus*) means "tooth walker" and describes one of the many uses to which the tusks are put. Wielding them like an ice pick, a walrus can anchor its tusks into an ice floe in order to clamber out of the water. The tusks are also used to drag the animal's heavy body along the ocean floor as it feeds on clams and other shellfish in the mud. The tusks make fearsome weapons. Bull walruses use their tusks to threaten other bulls during the breeding season. Both sexes use the tusks to defend themselves against predators—polar bears and killer whales.

Walruses are rarely found alone. They spend most of the day sleeping on rocky beaches or ice floes, huddled together. They are nomads, with no fixed homes. Throughout the year, they travel in jostling, bellowing, snorting herds of up to a hundred animals, cruising slowly around the north polar seas along with the ice floes.

THE SPECIES OF PINNIPEDS

SPECIES	WHERE THEY LIVE
TRUE SEALS	
Harbor seal	Coasts of North America, Northern Europe, Northeastern Asia
Ringed seal	Arctic, North Atlantic, Baltic Sea
Baikal seal	Lake Baikal
Caspian seal	Caspian Sea
Ribbon seal	Bering Sea
Harp seal	Arctic and North Atlantic
Gray seal	Northeastern North America, Northern Europe
Bearded seal	Arctic
Crabeater seal	Antarctica
Ross seal	Antarctica
Leopard seal	Antarctica and Subantarctic islands
Weddell seal	Antarctica
Mediterranean monk seal	Mediterranean and Aegean seas
Hawaiian monk seal	Northwestern Hawaiian islands
Hooded seal	Arctic, Northeastern North America
Southern elephant seal	Subantarctic islands, Southern South America
Northern elephant seal	Western North America
EARED SEALS	
South African fur seal	Southwest Africa
South American fur seal	South America
Australian fur seal	Southern Australia
Tasmanian fur seal	Tasmania
New Zealand fur seal	New Zealand
Kerguelen fur seal	Antarctica
Guadalupe fur seal	Guadalupe (off Baja California)
Northern fur seal	North Pacific
California sea lion	West coast of North America
Steller's sea lion	North Pacific
South American sea lion	South America, Galapagos
Australian sea lion	Islands off West Australia
New Zealand sea lion	Southern islands of New Zealand
WALRUS	
Walrus	Arctic

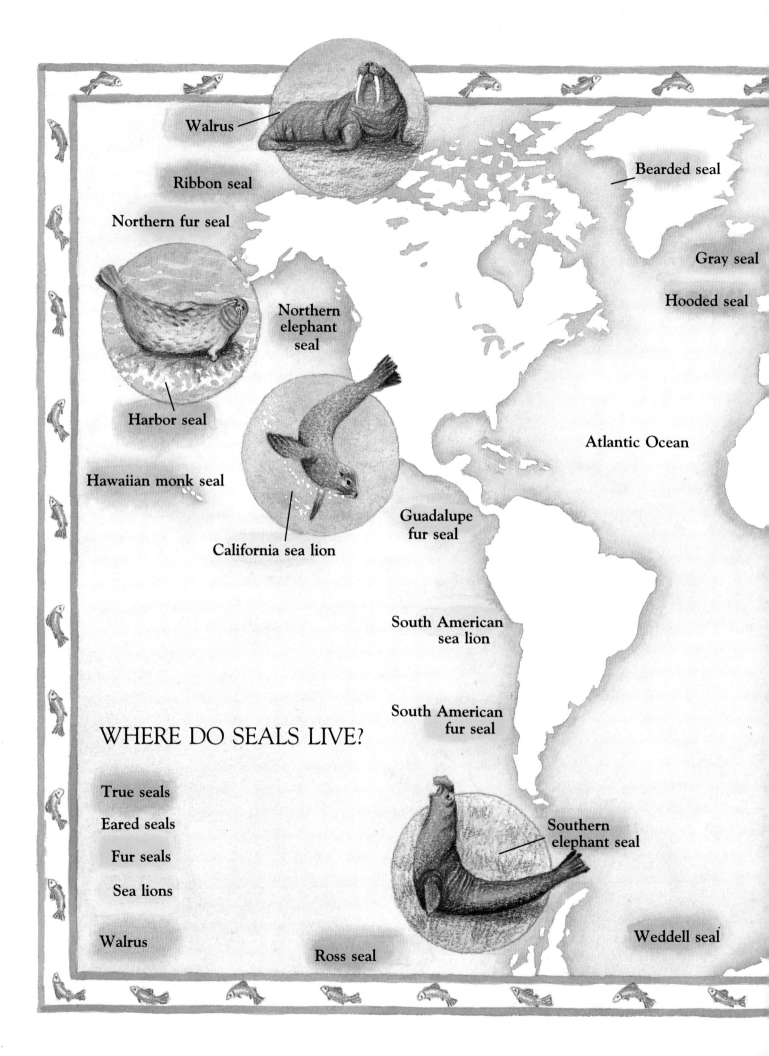

Walrus

Ribbon seal

Northern fur seal

Bearded seal

Gray seal

Hooded seal

Northern
elephant
seal

Harbor seal

Atlantic Ocean

Hawaiian monk seal

Guadalupe
fur seal

California sea lion

South American
sea lion

South American
fur seal

WHERE DO SEALS LIVE?

True seals

Eared seals

Fur seals

Sea lions

Walrus

Ross seal

Southern
elephant
seal

Weddell seal

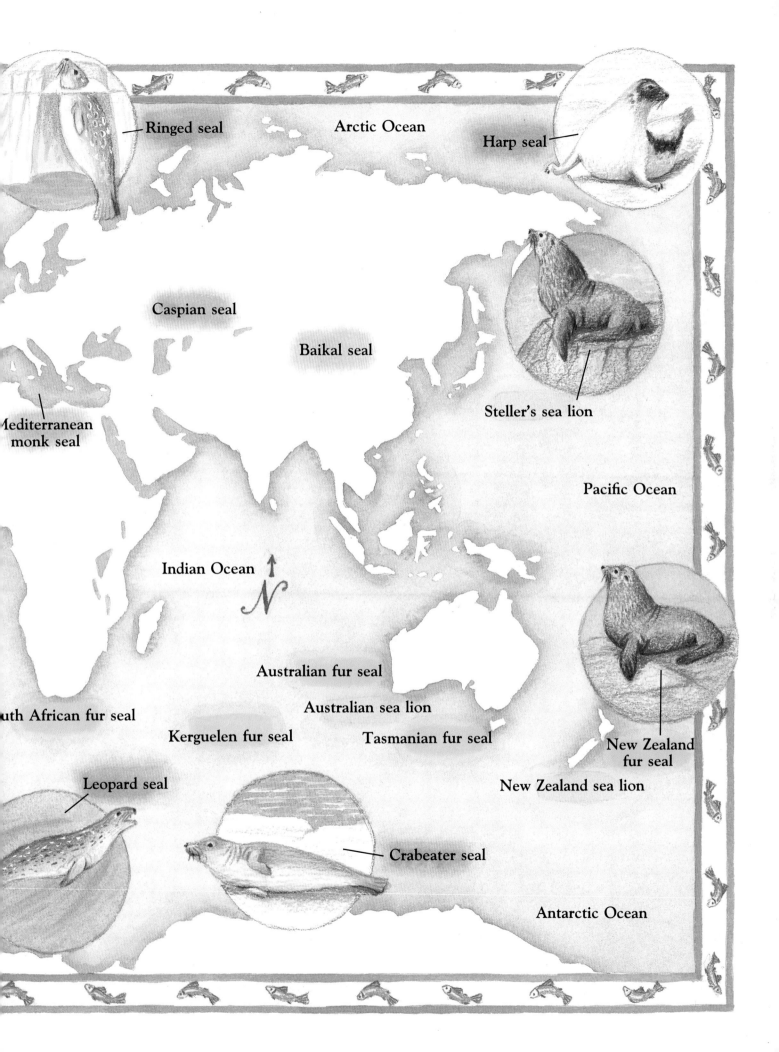

Ringed seal

Arctic Ocean

Harp seal

Caspian seal

Baikal seal

Steller's sea lion

Mediterranean monk seal

Pacific Ocean

Indian Ocean ↑ N

Australian fur seal

South African fur seal

Kerguelen fur seal

Australian sea lion

Tasmanian fur seal

New Zealand fur seal

New Zealand sea lion

Leopard seal

Crabeater seal

Antarctic Ocean

Seasons of a Seal

The lives of all eared seals and many true seals revolve around the yearly breeding season, when they gather on land in colonies, called *rookeries*. They assemble in the same places, year after year. Some of these gatherings are spectacular, numbering hundreds of thousands of seals.

During the breeding season, seal cows give birth to a single pup, then the males and females mate to produce offspring for the next year. The length of the breeding season and the time of year a species breeds depend a lot on the climate. Most kinds of seals give birth to their young in the late winter or early spring.

Most species of true seals have short breeding seasons, especially those that live in very cold areas. Their pups grow quickly, and some are weaned (no longer dependent on their mother's milk) as early as three weeks after they are born! The parents and their young do not stay together as families. In some species, the females gather in a separate group from the males while raising the pups. In others, adult bulls and cows form small, scattered groups. Shortly after the pups are weaned, the adults and young disperse back into the ocean.

Eared seals and the larger true seal species have longer breeding seasons. They form groups within the rookeries, each group consisting of a single bull and anywhere from seven to seventy cows. Each bull competes with other bulls, defending the small area of land where his cows are gathered. The mother seals may suckle and look after their pups for up to five months before the colony breaks up and the seals part company. Some of these seals spend the rest of the year in the ocean, swimming hundreds or thousands of miles from their breeding places. The yearly

This New Zealand fur seal pup should be able to look after itself by the time it is five months old.

gathering at the breeding sites helps make sure that they can find each other again to reproduce.

Most of what we know about pinnipeds comes from studying their life on land. Very little is known about their life at sea because it is much more difficult to observe them there. Many years of patient watching, measuring, and recording are needed before some of the mysteries of a seal's life can be unraveled. Where do seals go in winter? What do they eat? How much do they eat? How quickly do they grow? How long do they live? For many species, the answers to even such simple questions as these are not known. One species for which we do know the answers is the northern fur seal, whose amazing life story follows.

A northern fur seal bull guards his territory on the Pribilof Islands.

BREEDING BEACHES

In mid-April, the thick sea ice in the Arctic begins to break up. Pushing their way past the floating rafts of ice in the North Pacific Ocean, bull fur seals head northward. They swim toward two remote pinpoints of rock that jut out of the chilly waters west of Alaska. The tiny islands that draw the seals onward are named the Pribilof Islands, after the Russian sea captain who discovered them in 1786. Soon, the cold and empty beaches of these islands will become arenas for one of the biggest and most dramatic gatherings of animals to be seen anywhere in the world.

Older bulls, seven years of age or more, are first to arrive at the islands. They cautiously clamber from the sea onto the rocky shores and prepare to stake their claims to the land. From then on, each bull will try to guard his bit of the coast against all other bulls. Only the strongest will still have places on the beach when the female seals arrive a few weeks later. Only those with the most endurance will become the fathers of next year's pups. The unsuccessful bulls — those that are too young, too old, or too weak to hold a territory — will be forced farther and farther inland, or to other parts of the island. The other bulls will not allow them to breed this year.

Northern fur seals are magnificent animals. The bulls are more than six feet long and weigh between 400 and 600 pounds. They look majestic in their thick fur coats with short manes covering their massive shoulders. They have spent the winter at sea in sheltered bays to the south, feeding on plentiful supplies of fish and squid. Now in peak condition, they face the prospect of nearly three months on land without food or rest. They will have no time to go fishing in the ocean or to sleep in the weak spring sunshine. Until the breeding season starts to wind

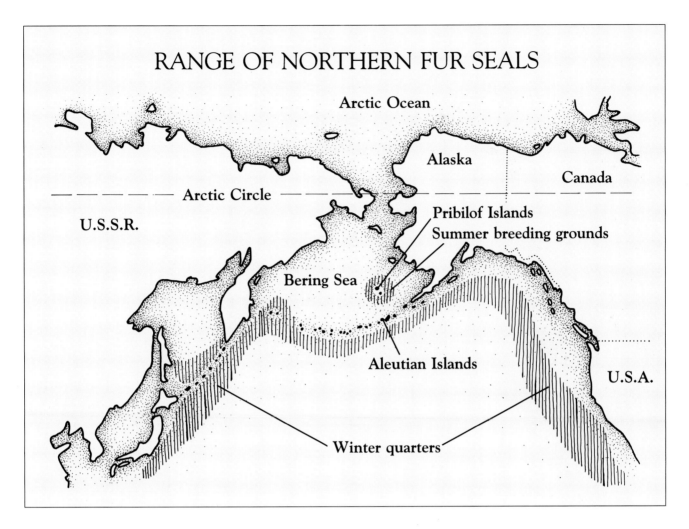

RANGE OF NORTHERN FUR SEALS

Arctic Ocean

Alaska

Canada

Arctic Circle

U.S.S.R.

Pribilof Islands
Summer breeding grounds

Bering Sea

Aleutian Islands

U.S.A.

Winter quarters

down in late summer, the bulls will spend all their energy guarding against rivals.

Every day brings more bulls to the islands, and soon there are hundreds of them packed onto the sand-and-gravel beaches. Each bull defends a small territory. Some territories are only two or three times the area occupied by the animal, and the biggest extend no more than fifteen feet in any direction from where it sits. From within these tiny kingdoms, the bulls watch each other warily and roar warnings to their neighbors. The earliest and biggest bulls take the best places — the front rows along the edge of the sea. They will be first to greet the arriving cows. But now they are lined up facing inland, watching for challenges from ambitious bulls in less favorable parts of the beach. Of all the bull seals gathered on the islands, only about two-thirds will be able to keep territories. The rest of the bull seals gather in non-territorial groups.

27

As May draws to an end, the restless bulls bellow at one another more often. Usually, a bull's noisy threats put off possible intruders into his territory. Sometimes, however, bluster isn't enough, and rival bulls come to blows. They lunge and snap at each other, trying to grip their opponent by the neck. They shove and chase and bite, scattering blood and fur on the sand as they fasten their sharp teeth into rolls of flesh. Fights can last twenty minutes or more, and staying power is one key to success. The losers are chased into the sea or through the pack of nearby bulls, who take up a chorus of roars. Most of the territory-holders have scars on their bodies, signs of bloody battles in earlier years.

The female fur seals reach the Pribilof Islands in June. They have been farther south than the males over the winter, many of them as far as the waters off the coast of southern California. As with the bulls, the older and more experienced females arrive first. They tend to go back to exactly the same place on the same beach that they used the year before. The cows outnumber the bulls by about forty to one. As the cows leave the sea to join their mates, the herds on the beaches quickly swell into the tens of thousands.

The females' arrival causes great excitement as each bull tries to gather a number of cows around him. The strongest bulls may hold as many as seventy, but the average group consists of one bull and twenty to thirty cows.

Within a day or two of landing on the islands, each mature cow gives birth to a single pup. The mothers became pregnant almost exactly one year before. However, the fertilized egg has not taken the whole year to develop into a pup. For four months

WHY DO THEY ROAR?

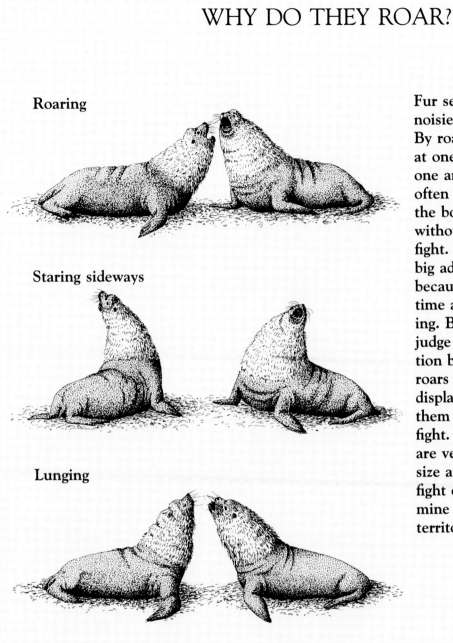

Roaring

Staring sideways

Lunging

Fur seals and sea lions are the noisiest of the pinnipeds. By roaring, staring sideways at one another, or lunging at one another, the bulls can often settle quarrels over the boundaries of territories without actually having to fight. Avoiding fights is a big advantage for the bulls, because it leaves them more time and energy for breeding. Bulls may be able to judge one another's condition by the loudness of their roars and the vigor of their displays. Perhaps this tells them which bull would win a fight. Only when two bulls are very closely matched in size and strength will they fight one another to determine which one keeps the territory.

after mating, the tiny ball of cells that was to become a fur seal was held resting inside its mother's womb. Then, during the fifth month, it suddenly began growing and developing. This delay in the embryo's growth makes sure that the pup is born when the fur seals make their yearly visit to the breeding beaches, and not earlier, while its mother is still far away at sea.

More than one and a half million
fur seals gather on the Pribilof
Islands each year to breed.

SUMMER SCHOOL

The ten-pound pup is born headfirst on the muddy shore, inside the territory of one of the bulls. It is clothed in dense, black fur and its eyes are fully open. The mother fur seal sniffs and prods the baby with her nose. The wet, velvety pup responds with a bleat. Both the smell and the sound of her baby will help the mother find it later in the summer, after it has wandered to join the thousands of other pups born to other mothers all over the beach.

Above the crash of the surf, you can hear the herd's hullabaloo from far away. It sounds like an excited crowd at a concert or sports arena. Pups cry to their mothers who respond with barks, snorts, and grunts. Bulls bellow back and forth. Mobs of screaming gulls hover and fight over scraps on the beach. There is urgency in the noise and urgency in the pups' lives. They must grow and learn quickly, because by the fall they will be on their own.

The pup snuggles close to the warmth of its mother's body and soon discovers one of the four black nipples hidden deep within the fur on her belly. Like all mammals, young fur seals are nourished by their mothers' milk until they are old enough to eat other food. The pup suckles hungrily. Then it falls into a deep sleep, its stomach full.

During its first few days, the pup's life consists of little more than sleeping and feeding. Its mother's rich milk contains more than forty percent fat, which the pup needs to give it enough warmth and energy to survive. Within a week, the pup has already grown noticeably bigger. Now the mother seal herself is hungry. She has remained on the beach since her pup was born, and it is time for her to return to the sea and feed. As long as she is suckling the pup, she must eat enough food for the two of them. Leaving her pup asleep among the pebbles and seaweed, she dodges her way through the crowded beach and eagerly plunges into the waves.

The cow may spend up to ten days at sea, diving for fish in the deep waters many miles from the breeding beach. She swims slowly and steadily, saving bursts of speed for chasing schools of silvery herring or sardines. Gorging on fish, and with time to rest, she soon regains strength.

Her pup, meanwhile, begins exploring on its own. Flopping across the stones and sand near the water's edge, it joins other pups whose mothers have also gone fishing. They play together in large groups, splashing in pools and tugging at bits of seaweed and other debris stranded on the beach. Their play is serious business, giving them the skills they will need for swimming, hunting, and fighting.

Each fur seal mother returning from a fishing trip can pick out her own baby from the thousands on the beach. She locates it first by sound and then, when closer, by smell. A mother feeds only her own pup and will ignore the cries of other hungry pups nearby. If a cow is killed by a predator or an accident during these few weeks, her pup, too, will starve and die.

After the cow and pup are reunited, the hungry youngster fastens onto one of its mother's nipples and bloats itself on her milk. The mother fur seal stays on the beach near her pup for another couple of days, letting it suckle frequently. Then she turns her back on her growing offspring and heads out to sea once more, joining thousands of other mothers in a busy flow of seals coming and going between the islands and the ocean fishing grounds. The cow repeats the pattern—seven to ten days of fishing followed by two days of nursing—throughout the summer.

Biologists have discovered that this cycle of nursing affects the growth of the baby fur seal's teeth.

When the pup is not feeding, its teeth stop growing. This makes a permanent record of the feeding pattern that a fur seal carries for life. Just as you can look at the thickness of the rings in a tree trunk to find out how much the tree grew each year, so the bands of light and dark ivory in the roots of a fur seal's teeth show how much the animal was feasting and fasting as a pup.

By the time they are five weeks old, the pups have learned how to swim. As they paddle in the shallow coves, they discover the sights, sounds, and smells of the ocean that will soon become their second home. They feel the surging of the waves and glimpse the darting sealife that they must learn how to catch. They encounter other seals in the herd and learn about the social life of their species. They also come to know danger. There are rough seas, sharks, and killer whales. Pups that venture too far too soon may not make it back. Some get lost and starve to death. Others become exhausted and drown. Many of the pups stumble through their short, risky infancy. Many others do not survive it.

The rich seas that give northern fur seals their food also hold the danger of storms and predators.

One of the earliest hazards in the pups' lives is their own fathers. On the crowded beaches, a half-ton bull fighting a neighbor or chasing a cow is not likely to notice a small pup underfoot. Pups get crushed by accident or are carelessly picked up and tossed away by a frustrated bull.

A less dramatic but equally deadly threat comes from the pups' mothers. More precisely, it comes from their mothers' milk. In the fat around the cow's milk glands live hundreds of tiny parasites called *hookworms*. Almost all fur seals are affected. In the adult fur seals, these parasites are not active. The hookworms are resting during the early, or *larval*, stage of their life and do not cause any harm. The larvae get into the cow's milk, however, and pass from her into the stomach of her pup. There they change into adult hookworms. The hookworms attach their hooks to the pup's intestines. Later they drill through the intestinal wall, causing internal bleeding that may kill the pup.

Thousands of young fur seals die this way every year. Those that survive until they no longer drink their mother's milk will never have to face this threat again. But in a few years' time, when the female pups become mothers, they will, in turn, pass the hookworm larvae to their own offspring.

The killer whale is one of the main predators of the northern fur seal.

By the end of the short northern summer, the huge, noisy seal rookeries begin to break up. Although a few young females may still arrive at the islands to give birth as late as the end of August, most of the breeding activity is over. With fewer cows to fight over, the bulls are quieter. They can now take naps, or drag their hungry, wrinkled bodies down the beach to slosh in the surf. After two months of breeding duty, a bull may have lost as much as sixty pounds. He is no longer the fine, sleek creature he was in May or June. The "bachelor" males—those who didn't breed—loll and fish in small groups at sea. They have not been tied to the land and look in better shape than the bulls who chased them from their territories weeks before. They will have another chance at being fathers next season.

At about two months, the baby fur seal begins to shed its first coat.

WINTER AT SEA

Two months after its birth, the northern fur seal pup has more than doubled its weight. It is now a plump twenty-two pounds. The velvety black coat the pup was born with is beginning to molt. Now the pup spends a lot of its time scratching. In another month, the coat will be replaced by a handsome silver-gray one. The black coat of babyhood is a simple layer of

35

hair fibers, like the fur of a cat or dog. But the new silver coat will have a different structure, designed to keep the pup warm and dry in the ice-cold ocean. It will have a thick underfur of fine fibers and a longer outer fur of stiff, waterproof hairs that give the seal its smooth, sleek appearance.

The adult seals, too, are molting. Millions of old hairs, blunted and damaged by months of fighting and crawling over pebbles and rocks, must be shed. New hairs grow in their place, preparing the seals to leave the land and spend the winter at sea. Growing a new coat uses a lot of energy. The bulls, already exhausted by the breeding season, spend much of these fall days in deep sleep.

In September, rain storms come to the islands and the temperatures drop rapidly. The mother seal has been out on ten fishing trips and returned to her pup ten times. The pup is nearly four months old, and its last teeth are already growing in. The pup can get its own food now and no longer depends on its mother's milk.

Mid-October brings the first frost, and flakes of snow dust the beaches. The mother seal is restless, feeling the urge to swim south. She leaves the rookery on another fishing trip, but this time she will not return to her pup. She follows the currents and the coastlines in the wake of other seals. She chases schools of fish and squid farther and farther out into the ocean. She keeps on going, beginning the 3,000-mile journey that will take her to her winter quarters.

The pup, now a sturdy thirty-five pounds, is on its own. As the pup's hunger grows, it calls and searches for its mother among the many cows still on the beach. Not finding her, the pup follows others into the bay and greedily snaps up some of the swarming shrimps and tiny fish that gather there.

At the end of the breeding season, Northern fur seals, like this adult bull, again lead mostly solitary lives as hunters.

The dark days drag into November, and more and more seals abandon the islands to retrace their long voyages through the Pacific Ocean. Before long, the pups will also depart, leaving behind for the first time the familiar beaches where they were born. By month's end, the islands are deserted. The sound of a seal will not be heard here again until nearly six months have passed.

With the end of the breeding season, the social life of the fur seals is over for the year. It is only on land that the seals gather together in large herds. At sea, they travel and hunt alone, or in twos and threes. Sometimes, small groups collect in places where fish are plentiful, but they separate when the food is gone. The cows, bulls, and pups take different paths from the islands. By late winter, the Pribilof seals are scattered throughout the vast Pacific Ocean.

The cows, which were first to leave the breeding beaches, migrate the farthest south. They pass the entire winter and spring on the open ocean, rarely coming within sight of land. They travel and feed at night, diving up to 300 feet deep after fish and squid. During the day they rest on the water, floating at the surface with only their noses and flippers in the air. Air bubbles trapped in their dense fur give the seals extra buoyancy. By late January, the cows are at their winter journey's end, somewhere in the ocean between San Francisco Bay and Baja California.

The older bulls stay in the sheltered waters near Alaska for the winter. Food is plentiful here, and thick layers of fat insulate their bodies, keeping them warm. The closer to the breeding islands they remain, the sooner they can return the next spring, and the better their chances of getting a good territory.

The pups, which are now four to six months old, must face their first winter at sea without any help from their parents. It is a harsh challenge, and many do not survive. They spread southward along the coastline, protected from the worst of the winter storms that lash the open seas. Still not expert at hunting and able to capture only smaller prey, they lose weight.

Bulls regain all their lost weight over the winter, putting on sixty pounds or more. By early spring, they are ready to return to the Pribilof Islands and set up their territories on the beaches.

The cows begin their return journey to the islands in February. They cruise northward at a leisurely pace, often in the company of dolphins, seabirds, and other seals going to the Arctic to breed. Cows begin breeding as young as three to five years of age and may give birth to six or more pups over the course of their lives.

More than half the pups born during the summer will die before spring arrives. Those that live will

weigh little more at a year than they did at four months, when they first left the land. After wintering among the islands off the coast of British Columbia, the pups follow the ocean currents out into the Pacific. They spend the summer far out at sea, hunting and growing. In the fall of their second year, at about fifteen months of age, the young seals finally return to the beach where they were born. They stay on the fringe of the colony each breeding season, until they are old enough to take part in producing their own pups.

Fur seal cows live apart from males except in the summer breeding season.

Life in the Cold

The harp seal gets its name from the harp-shaped marking on its back. Adults are about six feet long and weigh up to 400 pounds.

Imagine spending most of your life lying on slabs of ice on a frozen sea. That's what harp seals do. These sleek animals live in the chilly North Atlantic Ocean, on the opposite side of North America from the northern fur seals. Like the fur seals, harp seals are great travelers. They move down and up the ocean between northern Greenland and the Gulf of St. Lawrence, following the sea ice as it builds up and shrinks with the seasons. Harp seals are usually found far out to sea among drifting ice floes, or on the jagged piles of ice and frozen snow at the edges of the ice sheets. They even give birth to their pups on ice — in the middle of winter! Because of this, harp seals have been given the scientific name *Pagophilus*, meaning "ice-lover."

Adult harp seals have the typical plump, tapered shape of true seals. Unlike fur seals, male and female harp seals are about the same size. They spend their summers swimming and hunting north of the Arctic Circle. In October, when the ocean starts to freeze over, the seals journey slowly southward. The females finally gather for the winter on the ice around Newfoundland and the Labrador coast of eastern Canada. Here, hundreds of thousands of harp seal cows haul themselves out of the sea and onto the ice. The bulls form separate groups, several miles farther north. From January to March, the harp seals make their home on this frozen desert of ice with its bitterly cold temperatures, fierce winds, and drifting snow. In late February and early March, their pups are born.

The sea ice in winter seems like a terrible place and time for an animal to have its young. But harp seals are well adapted to these harsh conditions. At birth, a harp seal pup weighs between fifteen and twenty pounds and is covered with long, white, fluffy

fur. With its large, round eyes and dark muzzle, it has an appealing, soulful look. For the first week of its life, the mother stays close to her pup's side. This helps to keep the pup warm and allows it to suckle from her frequently. The mother seal's milk is about ten times richer in fat than cow's milk. On this diet, the baby seal is one of the fastest-growing mammals. At only two weeks old, a pup may be close to eighty pounds — over four times its weight at birth.

The seal pup needs this rapid gain in size to protect it from the cold: a small animal loses heat to the outside more rapidly than a large animal. The pup also keeps warm by shivering. This works its body's

Herds of female harp seals gather along the edges of ice floes to have their pups.

41

HARP SEAL MIGRATION

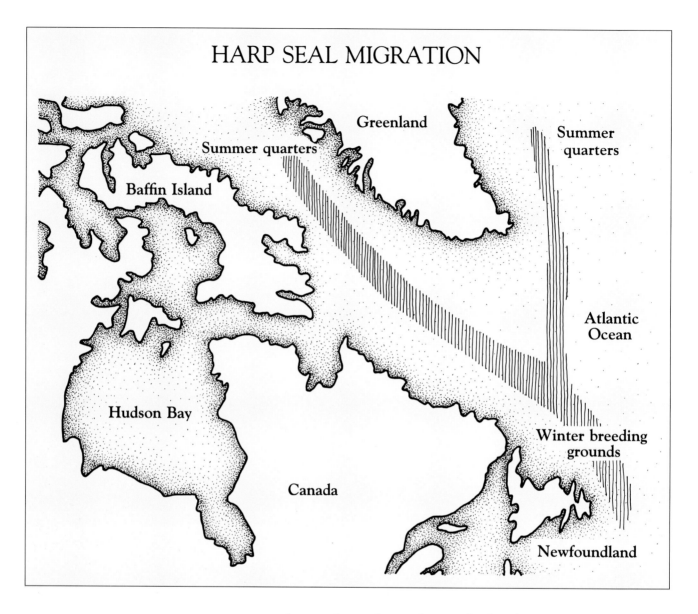

Greenland

Summer quarters

Summer quarters

Baffin Island

Atlantic Ocean

Hudson Bay

Winter breeding grounds

Canada

Newfoundland

muscles and produces heat. A third way it protects itself from the cold is by having a special type of fat in its body, called *brown fat*, which can produce heat from food very quickly. Animals that hibernate for the winter in northern areas, such as chipmunks and groundhogs, also have this type of fat.

Adult harp seals are even better protected against the cold than their pups. Like all true seals, an adult harp seal has several inches of blubber under its skin to keep its body warmth inside and the cold outside. The blubber makes up from one-third to nearly a half of an adult true seal's total weight. The blubber acts like insulation in a building, forming a barrier that does not conduct much heat. Measurements made by scientists have shown that a seal swimming in freezing sea water, with a temperature of 29 degrees Fahrenheit, has a body temperature of 99 degrees Fahrenheit only an inch and a half below its skin.

The excellent insulation provided by the fat is helped by another characteristic of the seal — its shape. As you may have experienced, body heat is lost especially quickly through extremities such as fingertips, toes, ears, and noses. These are the first parts to get frostbitten on a cold day. True seals have less of a problem with this because of their streamlined shape, with no projecting ears or noses. The most exposed parts of their bodies are the flippers. To reduce the amount of heat lost from the flippers to the cold surroundings, seals have a modified system of blood vessels in their flippers (see diagram and explanation in the box on page 44).

Baby harp seals grow rapidly on their mothers' fat-rich milk.

HOW DO SEALS KEEP WARM?

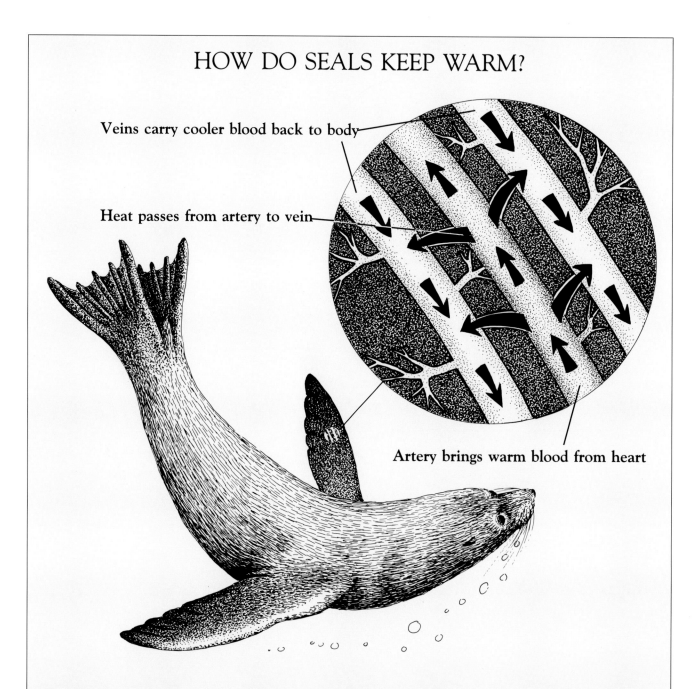

Veins carry cooler blood back to body

Heat passes from artery to vein

Artery brings warm blood from heart

The blood pumped from the seal's heart is the same warm temperature as the internal organs. However, when the blood flows near the seal's body surface — through the skin and flippers — it loses some of this heat to the outside.

To reduce the heat loss, the blood vessels form a tight network where they pass from the seal's body into its flippers. Each *artery* (a blood vessel carrying warm blood from the heart) is closely surrounded by a number of *veins* (blood vessels carrying cooler blood from the body surface). Because the vessels run close together, some of the warmth from the arteries that might otherwise be lost to the sea is "captured" by the veins instead and goes back into the deeper parts of the body. In this way, the animal doesn't lose a lot of heat or use up energy trying to keep its flippers warm.

Other sea-living mammals, such as porpoises and whales, also have blood vessels that are modified in this same way.

A harp seal "whitecoat" pup at two weeks of age looks weak and helpless. By four weeks of age, however, this pup's coat will turn gray, and the young seal will be ready to look after itself.

Fur seals also have coats with a unique design that keeps them warm and dry in the cold water. A fur seal's coat has two layers. Next to the skin is a dense *underfur*, in which hairs are arranged in bundles of twenty or more. These hairs are so fine that more than 300,000 of them crowd onto every square inch of the seal's body. The hairs are curly and form a tight mesh that contains billions of microscopic air spaces. These tiny pockets of air trap heat and also help keep out the cold water. Projecting above the underfur are longer, stiffer *guard hairs*. They make up an outer layer of fur that completely covers the underfur. Glands at the base of each hair bundle produce oil that makes the outer hairs water-repellent. Even when a fur seal is diving, its skin under the fur layers always stays dry. The two hair layers together act rather like a combination rubber wet suit and wool coat. No wonder fur seals look comfortable while lazing in the northern oceans in January!

A seal's behavior adapts it for life in the cold as ably as its well-padded body does. For example, harp seals must keep small areas of the sea from freezing over so they can get underwater to feed or to escape polar bears—and they must be able to get out of the sea again afterward. They do this by grouping in large numbers around holes or channels in the ice and regularly entering and leaving the water. Their frequent comings and goings prevent new ice from building up.

At the other end of the world, near the South Pole, Weddell seals solve the problems of a frozen ocean in a different way. They are hardy animals that spend the entire winter *under* the ice. This has two advantages for them. Their main predators are air-breathing killer whales, which will not swim very far under the ice to catch them. Also, sea water in the winter is far warmer than the sub-zero Antarctic air. In order to breathe, Weddell seals find air pockets trapped between the sea surface and the ice. In addition, they can use their teeth like can openers to cut breathing holes in the ice. To do this, they fasten their lower jaws into the ice, then revolve in a circle until their projecting upper teeth rasp their way through. This method puts a great strain on their teeth, which become very worn in older seals.

The small ringed seals of the Arctic also use ice and snow to their advantage. In April and May, expectant mothers dig out long, low caves in the deep snow that has drifted up onto the ice. One end of the cave is usually up against the piled-up ice, while the opposite end has a hole in the floor that acts as a doorway to the sea. These caves make safe and cozy places for the seals to have their pups—hidden away from the bitter weather and out of sight of their predators.

HOW DO PINNIPEDS KEEP COOL
WHEN IT'S HOT?

With all their insulation from fat and fur, pinnipeds have no problem with the cold. But what about the heat? How do they keep from getting too hot while basking in the sun, or after a period of strenuous activity?

When seals need to lose body heat, the blood vessels near their skin and in their flippers expand, so more blood flows into them. The heated blood quickly cools as it flows near the body surface. Some seals help the cooling process by fanning their flippers back and forth through the air.

Elephant seals and walruses, with their large, bulky bodies, have a particular problem getting rid of extra heat. Elephant seals some-times flick sand over their bodies with their flippers to keep the sun off their bare skin. In walruses, the blood vessels near the wrinkly skin expand and fill with blood, flushing the skin and turning it into a "radiator." A herd of hot walruses makes a spectacular sight as they glow reddish-pink under the clear Arctic sky.

Life in the Deep

How long can you hold your breath? Maybe for up to a minute, if you're good at it. But many seals, with lungs no bigger than a human adult's, can easily stay underwater without breathing for twenty minutes or more. They need this ability in order to dive in search of their food. They also need to stand up to the high pressure on their bodies under hundreds of feet of water. To deal with these problems, seals have several amazing adaptations, most of which cannot be seen from the outside.

To prepare for a dive, a seal keeps its nostrils and earholes closed. Then, unlike you or me, it breathes *out* before it dives. All the oxygen it will need while underwater is carried in its blood and muscles, rather than in its lungs. A seal has about one and a half to two times as much blood in its body as a land-living mammal of similar size. This large amount of blood helps it store a large amount of oxygen before diving. The Weddell seal, for example, can store about five times as much oxygen in its blood as a person can.

As soon as the seal's head dips below the water, a series of changes inside the seal's body is triggered automatically. These changes all help the body use its oxygen supply in the most efficient way.

The seal's heartbeat slows at once, from about one hundred beats per minute to about ten beats per minute. This slows the rate of blood circulation through the seal's body. However, the seal must keep up the oxygen supply to its essential organs, such as the heart and brain, or they will be damaged. To allow this, the flow of blood to some other parts of its body is greatly reduced. The seal's kidneys stop operating during the dive, and its muscles can work without oxygen from the blood.

As the oxygen in the seal's body is used up, waste carbon dioxide is produced. The seal's body does not react to this gas in the same way a human body does. In people, a build-up of carbon dioxide in the blood automatically makes us breathe in. But a seal can tolerate high levels of this gas during a dive without any harmful effects.

When it comes back to the surface after a dive, the seal has one more handy adaptation. It can breathe out and in very rapidly, almost completely emptying its lungs of waste gas and breathing in new lungfuls of fresh air. With each breath, it exchanges ninety percent of the air in its lungs. People, by comparison, change only twenty percent of the air in their lungs with each breath.

Seals, like this harp seal, close their nostrils before they dive.

As any diver knows, the deeper underwater you go, the greater the pressure on your body. A human diver in a diving suit cannot dive much below 250 feet without running into great danger. The high pressure at this depth can collapse air spaces in the body, such as the lungs or ear cavities, and can even break ribs. The pressure also forces nitrogen gas from air in the body to be absorbed into the bloodstream. This leads to another problem when the diver comes back up. As the diver rises to the surface, the pressure falls. The dissolved nitrogen in the diver's body turns back into a gas. It forms bubbles in the blood vessels and joints—just as you get bubbles of gas forming in soda pop when you take the cap off the bottle and release the pressure. The bubbles of nitrogen in the diver's body cause pain (called "the bends") or even death.

How do seals meet these dangers, managing to survive dives of 1,000 feet or more? As has been mentioned, seals empty most of the air from their lungs before a dive. This gets rid of air space that might otherwise be crushed by pressure. Also, blood is pumped into the seal's ear cavities to drive out the air. Liquid cannot be squeezed as easily as air. In addition, a seal's ribs are very flexible, so they bend rather than break under pressure.

A seal does not get the bends because there is very little air, and therefore very little nitrogen, in its body during a dive. Furthermore, the air passages in its head and neck are lined with a material that does not let gases pass through it into the bloodstream. Around the seal's lungs, there is a special type of fat that can absorb and release nitrogen without producing bubbles. Thanks to all these remarkable adaptations, seals can dive and swim underwater in comfort.

When a seal is underwater, its nervous system has an automatic cut-off that prevents the seal from trying to breathe. Because of this, a seal can actually sleep underwater. The submerged sleeping seal will unconsciously surface to breathe every twenty minutes or so.

In addition to their lungs, walruses have two air pouches near the top of their windpipe, just below the throat. They can fill these pouches with air from their lungs, inflating them like a pair of water wings. The air pouches can stretch out to a huge size and are sealed off by a contracting muscle at their base. Scientists are not sure why walruses have these air sacs. They may help the animals stay afloat during their long journeys out at sea, when they cannot haul themselves out onto land or ice to rest. The native peoples of Alaska, who have observed walruses carefully, think that the pouches are used to magnify the sounds the walruses make — just as the hollow body of a drum magnifies the sound of the drum beat.

Seals can sleep while suspended in water, near the surface.

Underwater Hunters

The large, round eyes that give a seal its appealing look have a serious purpose. They are designed to help the seal find and catch its prey underwater. Even in the clearest water, it is hard to see more than about fifteen yards away. And only thirty feet down—just deep enough to cover a two- or three-story building—there is barely one-tenth the amount of light found at the surface. To help it see in such poor light conditions, a seal has mirror-like membranes at the backs of its eyes. These surfaces reflect and add to the light entering the seal's eyes. The *pupil*, or hole at the front of the eye, opens up wide when the seal is underwater, letting in as much light as possible. When the seal pops back into the bright light at the surface, the pupil rapidly shrinks again.

In seals, as well as in people, tiny glands at the inner corner of each eye produce *tears*. This liquid always covers your eyeballs, even when you are not crying. Tears form a thin film over the surface of the eyes that protects them and keeps them from drying out. In people, tear ducts between the eyes and nose drain away the liquid as more is produced by the glands. Seals do not have tear ducts. They do not need them because they spend most of their time in water, where the teardrops are washed away. For this reason, seals on land sometimes look as if they are crying, as their tears run out of their eyes and spill down their cheeks.

If you've ever opened your eyes while diving in a pool, you know that everything underwater looks blurred to you. That is because light waves passing into your eyes from the water bend by a different amount than light waves traveling to you through the air. If you wear goggles, trapping air against your eyes, everything looks clear again. Seals don't have this problem. The lenses inside their eyes are large and

round, like miniature crystal balls. These spherical lenses can sharply focus a wide range of light waves.

In murky water, at night, or at great depths, even the best eyes are not much help in hunting for prey. Seals also have a very good sense of touch, or feel. They don't even have to touch objects to "feel" them. Underwater, moving objects produce waves of pressure that spread out for a long distance around them — like the wake that spreads from a boat moving over the water's surface. Seals can detect these waves with their long, sensitive whiskers. The whiskers give the seal a sense of "distant touch." In addition to using this sense to find moving fish and other creatures in the dark, a seal can also use it to tell when it is swimming toward large solid objects. Pressure waves produced by the seal's own movement bounce off such objects and travel back to the seal's whiskers.

Seals use their eyes and whiskers to help them find their underwater prey.

WHAT DO SEALS EAT?

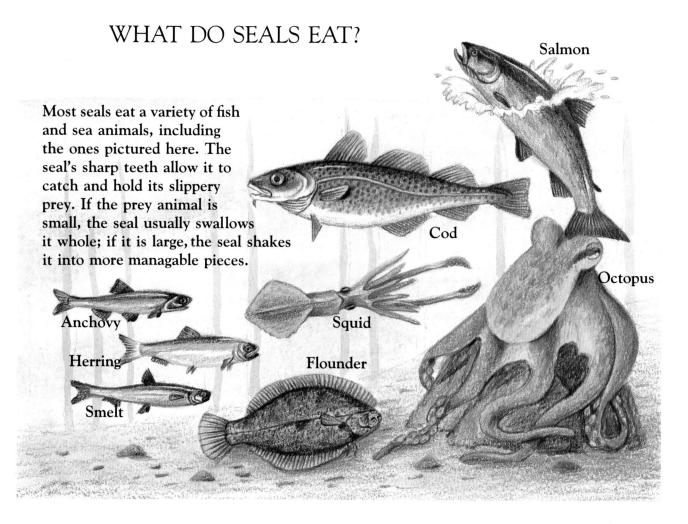

Most seals eat a variety of fish and sea animals, including the ones pictured here. The seal's sharp teeth allow it to catch and hold its slippery prey. If the prey animal is small, the seal usually swallows it whole; if it is large, the seal shakes it into more managable pieces.

Salmon

Cod

Octopus

Anchovy

Herring

Squid

Flounder

Smelt

Prey species hunted by most seals include squid, octopus, halibut, cod, flounder, sole, anchovies, herring, smelt, salmon, and other fish. Northern fur seals have wide-ranging taste: they are known to eat at least a hundred different types of prey. They catch fish that live on the deep sea floor as well as fish that swim in the sunlit waters near the surface.

Because it is difficult to watch seals feeding in the wild, biologists find out about what seals eat largely by studying what is in the stomachs of seals that have died. One interesting result of this was the discovery of a new species of fish. In the 1890s, biologists found a type of fish they had never seen before in the stomachs of northern fur seals. They didn't know what the fish were and named them "seal fish." No more studies of the seal fish were done until seventy years later, when biologists identified them as a type of smelt. These deep-sea fish have still never been seen alive.

To capture fish, seals have from thirty to thirty-six sharp, pointed teeth. When their jaws snap together, even the slipperiest fish has little chance of getting away. Seals grasp and tear at their prey, then swallow it whole. They have no teeth for chewing. They can eat underwater, but may bring larger fish to the surface to shake them into smaller pieces. A northern fur seal cow weighing sixty-five pounds eats about four to five pounds of fish each night. The entire colony of fur seals on the Pribilof Islands — about one and a half million animals — takes close to a million tons of fish and squid from the sea every year.

Seals digest their food very rapidly. A meal may pass through a seal's intestines in as little as six hours. Seals also have extremely long intestines for their size. A Steller's sea lion's intestines are reported to be more than 250 feet long when uncoiled — thirty-eight times the animal's body length. It is not known why they have such long intestines, although it may help them get energy from their food more efficiently.

The sharp teeth of this hooded seal show clearly that the seal is a predator.

Its thick whiskers help the bearded seal find food on the sea floor.

SPECIALIZED FEEDERS

Not all seals eat fish and squid. In fact, the most common seals in the world live on a very specialized diet. There may be more than five million *crabeater seals* that live in the waters around the Antarctic. Despite their name, they do not eat crabs but small shrimp-like animals, called *krill*. Explorers gave the crabeater its name because they thought the reddish fragments they saw in its droppings on the ice were bits of crab shells.

Crabeater seals are about nine feet long and weigh about 500 pounds. Krill are about two inches long. As you can imagine, each seal needs a lot of krill to survive. Fortunately, krill are so numerous that in some areas of the Antarctic there may be up to thirty-five pounds of them in every cubic yard of seawater.

In order to capture their tiny prey, crabeater seals have oddly shaped teeth that act like sieves, or strainers. Their upper teeth have long projecting points and their lower teeth fit into the spaces between these points. To eat, a crabeater seal takes in a mouthful of seawater containing krill. Then it partly closes its mouth and pushes the seawater out between its teeth. The krill are too big to get through this strainer and are trapped inside the seal's mouth.

Another specialized feeder is the *bearded seal*. Similar in size to the crabeaters, bearded seals live along shallow coasts in the Arctic. They need shallow water because they spend a lot of their time feeding on the sea floor. The long white whiskers for which they are named help the bearded seals find crabs, shrimp, and shellfish hidden in the mud and silt. Unlike many seals, bearded seals are unsociable. They are rarely seen near other seals, except during their short breeding season. They probably need a large space to themselves in order to find enough food. Bearded seals

have large claws on their front flippers, which they use to dig for their food. Like many seals, the bearded seal's stomach often contains mud and pebbles. These may be taken in by accident, or to act like a diver's weights, helping the animal stay down on the sea floor. Some scientists think that stones in the stomach may help with digestion, or stave off hunger pangs when food is scarce.

Those unusual pinnipeds of the Arctic, the walruses, can also be found digging on the ocean floor. They root for clams with their tusks, leaving churned mud and debris behind them. Many books about animals say that walruses crush clams and other shellfish with their teeth. However, their cheek teeth are weak. It is now thought that they suck the soft bodies of their prey out of their shells. A walrus may do this by holding the shell between its lips, forming its mouth into a cylinder, then moving its tongue back and forth like a piston to create strong suction. The empty shells are spat back into the sea. Some walruses hunt larger prey. They have been known to use their tusks to attack and kill seals, small beluga whales, and even other walruses.

Walruses use their tusks to dig for clams, mussels, starfish, crabs, and other small creatures that live on the sea floor.

Leopard seals kill and eat penguins and other seals.

Among the fiercest of all pinnipeds are the *leopard seals*. They live in the Antarctic, and eat mainly penguins and other seals. Like the big cats whose name they share, leopard seals are stealthy hunters. They often swim up to their prey from below, or lie hidden near the ice edge waiting for penguins to enter or leave the water. Leopard seals are large — up to ten feet and 900 pounds — and have especially large heads and jaws. In addition to catching their larger prey, they will also eat fish and squid, or scavenge the carcass of a whale.

HUNTERS OF SEALS

All pinnipeds are hunters. But pinnipeds are also hunted. Even the giant elephant seals and walruses have predators that attack their young. The animals that eat seals include large sharks, killer whales, polar bears, and, occasionally, wolves and other seals.

Polar bears in particular depend heavily on seal meat. During fall and winter, they travel for miles across the Arctic sea ice, following herds of seals on their seasonal migrations. Polar bears must catch the seals when they come up onto the ice. That is not so easy, since the seals usually stay close to a breathing hole. The bears' best chance is to creep up on a resting seal. That is probably why polar bears are white: it makes them hard for a seal to spot against the snow and ice. Another tactic, used by Arctic wolves as well as bears, is to lie in wait next to a seal's breathing hole and quickly grab the seal the moment it pokes its nose up.

Every year, bears, sharks, and killer whales eat thousands of seals. But another predator kills far more than all these hunters put together. The greatest threat to seals comes from human beings.

Slow-moving penguins are no match for the stealthy leopard seal.

Polar bears wait at seal breathing holes for their prey.

Pinnipeds and People

For centuries, people have hunted seals for their fur and meat. The Native peoples of the far north depended on seals for their survival and culture. Their traditional hunting methods, using hand-thrown harpoons, had little or no impact on the numbers of seals.

This situation changed when sealskin became widely popular for clothing, and when guns became widely available for hunting. Throughout the 1800s, fur traders in North America and Europe sold hundreds of thousands of seal pelts every year. The seal's habit of gathering on land in large herds during the breeding season made them easy prey. Using guns and explosives, sealers slaughtered huge numbers of seals. For example, between 1908 and 1910—only three years—hunters killed four million fur seals on the Pribilof Islands alone. Because of onslaughts such as this, some populations of seals were hunted to extinction.

Many seals are still hunted, but the numbers killed are now limited by laws. With this protection, seals such as the northern fur seal have increased in numbers. Today, however, pinnipeds are threatened by people in other ways than hunting. The coastal waters where they live are polluted by human-made wastes and poisons, washed in from rivers and land. Thousands of seals die each year after eating plastic garbage tossed from ships, or becoming entangled in fishing nets. Other seals are killed by oil spills. The threats that now face seals are threats to the ocean itself.

Pollution and overhunting have affected not only seals but many other ocean animals such as whales, dolphins, and some types of fish. Because many seals eat the same fish that people enjoy, fishermen and seals sometimes clash as they compete for this

shrinking food supply. Seals have been known to take fish right out of the fishermen's nets, damaging the nets as they bite through them.

Some people argue that the fish eaten by seals would otherwise be caught by fishermen. They say that if the number of seals were reduced, fishermen could catch more fish for people. Is this correct? In the past, the oceans of the world supported far larger numbers of both fish and seals. Native peoples who traditionally live on fish were able to catch thousands of salmon from areas only a few miles away from huge seal rookeries. Studies of seal feeding habits have found that seals may sometimes actually help salmon, trout, and other valuable fish by eating one of their enemies — the *lamprey*. These eel-like fish attach themselves to other fish and feed on their blood, eventually killing them.

In the natural balance of the underwater world, seals, fish, and all the other organisms that live together help one another to survive. For example, the droppings from seals add nutrients to the water that

Harp seal pups were killed by the hundreds of thousands until recently to meet the demand for fur clothes and sealskin products.

If the oceans aren't fit for this hooded fur seal pup to live in, we will suffer, too.

help microorganisms and plants to grow. The same thing happens when seals die naturally and their bodies decompose on the ocean floor or become food for scavenging crabs and small fish. In turn, the plants and small creatures of the sea are eaten by larger fish. Although seals eat fish, they are also part of a process that allows those same fish to grow. If people kill all the seals and other sea animals that compete for fish, they may find that the fish themselves will soon disappear as well.

The spectacular colonies of fur seals on the Pribilof Islands give us a rare chance to see and study a part of nature that has existed on the earth in remote areas for thousands of years. There are few unspoiled places like this left on the planet. These last wilderness areas are like international treasure houses — places where people can learn about some of the many other species with which we share our world. By saving such places and ways of life, animals such as these highly intelligent, fin-footed mammals may exist for a very long time.

INDEX

Numbers in italics refer to photographs.

Air bubbles, 38
Air passages, 50
Air pouches, 51
Alaska fur seals. *See* Northern fur seals
Ancestors, 11
Antarctic, 14, 46, 56, 58
Appearance
  harp seals, 40–41
  how to identify true seals and eared
    seals, 18–19
  molting, 35–36
  northern fur seal pup, 31
  walrus, 20
Arctic, 13, 20, 26, 56–57
Arctic wolves, 59
Artery, 44

Bearded seals, 56–57, 56
Birth
  fur seals, 28–29, 31
  harp seals, 40–41
  ringed seals, 46
Blood
  oxygen supply, 48–49
  vessels, 44, 47
Blubber, 42–43
Breathing, 48–51
Breathing holes, 46, 59
Breeding season, 24, 26–28, 35, 37, 60
Brown fat, 42
Bulls, 10
  breeding season, 24
  eared seals, 16
  elephant seals, 14
  harp seals, 40
  northern fur seals, 26–28, 26, 34–36,
    38
  ringed seals, 13
  sea lions, 16
  Steller's sea lion, 16
  walrus, 20
Buoyancy, 38

California sea lion, 16
Carbon dioxide, 49
Caribbean monk seal, 12
Carnivores, 6
Caves, ringed seals, 46
Coats, 35–36
  harp seal pup, 45

Cold
  adaptation for life in, 46
  fur seal's coat, 45
  protection against, 41–43
  reducing heat loss, 44
Cows, 10
  birth of fur seal pup, 28–29, 31
  breeding season, 24
  eared seals, 16
  harp seal, 40
  milk, 34
  northern fur seal, 28–29, 32, 38, 39,
    55
  nursing cycle, 32
  ringed seals, 13
  Steller's sea lion, 16
Crabeater seals, 56
Crawlers, 19

Diving, 48–51
Droppings, 61

Eared seals, 10, 11, 15–19
  appearance, 18
  breeding season, 24
  land movement, 19
  swimming, 19
  where they live, 21
Earless seals. *See* True seals
Ears, 18
Elephant seals, 14, 14, 47
Embryo, 28–29
Environment, 8
  eared seals, 15–17
  ringed seals, 13
  true seals, 12
Equator, 17
Extinction, 12, 60
Eyes, 52–53

Fall, northern fur seals, 36–37
Fat
  brown fat, 42
  surrounding lungs, 50
Families
  of pinnipeds, 10
  true seals, 24
Feeding habits
  help fish, 61
  leopard seals, 58
  northern fur seals, 32, 36, 38
  specialized diets, 56–57
  walruses, 57
Females. *See* Cows
Fights, 28, 29

Fins, 19
Fish, 54–55, 60–61
Fishing trips, northern fur seal cows, 32
Flippers, 19, 20, 43, 44, 47, 57
Fur seals, 10, 15, 17, 26. *See also*
    Northern fur seals
  breeding beaches, 26–29
  coat, 45
  growth of pup's teeth, 32–33
Fur traders, 60

Guadalupe fur seal, 17, *17*
Guard hairs, 45

Harp seals, 40–46, *40*, *41*, *43*, *45*, *49*,
    61
Harbor seals, 6–9, *7*, *8*, 10
Hazards to pups, 33–34
Heads, 18
Heat loss, 44, 47
Hibernating animals, 42
Hooded seals. *See* Monk seals
Hookworms, 34
Hunting
  by people, 60
  grounds, 8

Insulation, 38, 42–43
Intestines, 55

Killer whales, *34*, 46
Krill, 56

Lamprey, 61
Land, 8, 9, 25
  eared seals, 15
  fur seals, 37
  movement, 19
Leopard seals, 58, *58*
Limbs. *See* Flippers
Living areas. *See* Ranges
Lunging, 29
Lungs, 50

Males. *See* Bulls
Mammals, 10, 31, 41, 44
Migration
  fur seals, 36–38
  harp seals, 42
Milk, 34, 41
Molting, 35–36
Monk seals, 12, *55*, 62
Movement, 19

Native peoples, 60, 61
Necks, 18
Nervous system, 50
New Zealand fur seal, *25*

Nitrogen, 50
Nomads, 20
North American coasts, 14
North Atlantic Ocean, 40
Northern fur seals, 26, 30, 33, 37, 39
  breeding beaches, 26–29
  cows eating fish, 55
  feeding, 54
  population, 17
  pups, 28–29, 31–34, 35
  range, 27
  why do they roar, 29

Overhunting, 60
Oxygen, 48

Pacific coast, 8, 16, 17
Penguins, 58, 59
Pinnipeds, 9
  ancestors, 11
  roaring, 29
  species, 10, 21
Playing, 32
Polar bears, 58, 58
Pollution, 60
Predators, 8, 20, 34, 58–59
Pressure waves, 53
Pribilof Islands, 26, 28, 30, 38, 55, 60,
  62
Pupil, 52
Pups, 24
  growth of teeth, 32–33
  harp seal, 40–42, 49, 61
  northern fur seal, 28–29, 31–39

Ranges, 21–23, 27
Ringed seals, 13, 13, 46
Roaring, 27, 29
Rookeries, 24, 35

Salmon, 61
Sea, 8, 25
  eared seals, 15–17
  movement, 19
  natural balance of underwater world,
    61–62
  northern fur seals, 32, 33, 37–38
  true seals, 12–14
Sea lions, 10, 15–16, 15, 19, 29
Seals
  ancestors, 11
  bearded, 56–57
  breeding season, 24
  Caribbean monk, 12
  diving, 48–51
  eared, 10, 11, 15–19, 21, 24

elephant, 14, 47
environment, 8
eyes, 52–53
fur, 10, 15, 17, 26
Guadalupe fur, 17
harbor, 6–9, 10
harp, 40–46, 49, 61
identifying true and eared, 18–19
keeping cool when it's hot, 47
keeping warm, 44
leopard, 58
living areas, 21–23
monk, 12, 55, 62
New Zealand fur, 27
northern fur, 26–39
predators, 58–59
ringed, 13, 46
species, 10
threatened by people, 60–61
true, 10–14, 18–19
Weddell, 46, 48
where do they live, 22–23
whiskers, 53
Shape, true seal, 43
Shivering, 41
Size
  crabeater seals, 56
  eared seals, 16
  elephant seals, 14
  leopard seals, 58
  northern fur seals, 26
  ringed seals, 13
  Steller's sea lion, 16
Skin, ringed seal, 13
Sleeping, 51
Sounds, walrus, 51
Species, pinnipeds, 10, 21
Speed, sea lion, 16, 19
Spring, northern fur seals, 26–29
Staring, 29
Steller's sea lion, 16, 16, 55
Stomach, stones in, 57
Summer, northern fur seal pups,
  31–35, 39
Survival, northern fur seal pups,
  33–34, 38
Swimming, 19

Tears, 52
Teeth, 32–33, 46, 54, 55, 56
  crabeater seals, 56
  walrus, 57
Territories, 27–29
Touching, 53

Traveling, 7, 20, 38
  harp seals, 40
  northern fur seals, 38
True seals, 10–12, 12
  appearance, 18
  blubber, 42
  breeding season, 24
  land movement, 19
  shape, 43
  swimming, 19
  where they live, 21
Tusks, 20, 57

Underfur, 45
Underwater
  adaptations, 52–53
  natural balance of world, 61–62

Veins, 44

Walruses, 10, 11, 20, 20, 47, 47, 51, 57,
  57
Water. See Sea
Weaning, 24
Weddell seal, 46, 48
Weight
  blubber, 42
  elephant seals, 14
  leopard seals, 58
  northern fur seal pups, 31, 35, 38–39
  northern fur seals, 26, 55
  ringed seals, 13
Whiskers, 56
Winter
  harp seals, 40–43
  northern fur seals, 37–39
  spent under ice, 46